FRUITS YOU LOVE TO EAT
STRAWBERRIES

AMY CULLIFORD

A Crabtree Roots Book

Crabtree Publishing
crabtreebooks.com

School-to-Home Support for Caregivers and Teachers

This book helps children grow by letting them practice reading. Here are a few guiding questions to help the reader with building his or her comprehension skills. Possible answers appear here in red.

Before Reading:

• What do I think this book is about?
  • *I think this book is about how delicious strawberries are.*
  • *I think this book is about how to grow strawberries.*

• What do I want to learn about this topic?
  • *I want to learn why strawberries taste so good.*
  • *I want to learn if I can grow strawberries in my backyard.*

During Reading:

• I wonder why...
  • *I wonder why strawberry seeds are so small.*
  • *I wonder why strawberries are so juicy.*

• What have I learned so far?
  • *I have learned that strawberries are fruits.*
  • *I have learned that strawberries grow on plants.*

After Reading:

• What details did I learn about this topic?
  • *I have learned that strawberries change color as they grow.*
  • *I have learned that all strawberries have green leaves.*

• Read the book again and look for the vocabulary words.
  • *I see the word **plants** on page 6 and the word **leaves** on page 10. The other vocabulary words are found on page 14.*

Strawberries are **fruits**.

Strawberries come from little **seeds**.

The seeds grow in the ground and become **plants**.

As they grow, strawberries turn from green to white to red.

All strawberries have green **leaves**.

I like to eat strawberries!

Word List
Sight Words

all	green	little
and	ground	red
are	grow	the
become	have	they
come	I	to
eat	in	turn
from	like	white

Words to Know

fruits

leaves

plants

seeds

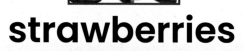

strawberries

38 Words

Strawberries are **fruits**.

Strawberries come from little **seeds**.

The seeds grow in the ground and become **plants**.

As they grow, strawberries turn from green to white to red.

All strawberries have green **leaves**.

I like to eat strawberries!

FRUITS YOU LOVE TO EAT
STRAWBERRIES

Written by: Amy Culliford
Designed by: Rhea Wallace
Series Development: James Earley
Proofreader: Melissa Boyce
Educational Consultant: Marie Lemke M.Ed.

Photographs:
Shutterstock: Nataly Studio: cover; pixahub: p. 1;
   Maria_Usp: p. 3; Nicole_P_Pix2017: p. 5; amenic181: p. 7;
   Alena Brozona: p. 9; MarcoFood: p. 11; Mokey Business
   Images: p. 13

Crabtree Publishing

crabtreebooks.com   800-387-7650
Copyright © 2024 Crabtree Publishing
All rights reserved. No part of this publication may be reproduced, stored in a retrieval system or be transmitted in any form or by any means, electronic, mechanical, photocopying, recording, or otherwise, without the prior written permission of Crabtree Publishing. In Canada: We acknowledge the financial support of the Government of Canada through the Canada Book Fund for our publishing activities.

Printed in Canada/122023/20231201

Published in Canada
Crabtree Publishing
616 Welland Ave.
St. Catharines, Ontario
L2M 5V6

Published in the United States
Crabtree Publishing
347 Fifth Ave
Suite 1402-145
New York, NY 10016

Library and Archives Canada Cataloguing in Publication
Available at Library and Archives Canada

Library of Congress Cataloging-in-Publication Data
Available at the Library of Congress

Hardcover: 978-1-0398-0972-7
Paperback: 978-1-0398-1025-9
Ebook (pdf): 978-1-0398-1131-7
Epub: 978-1-0398-1078-5